MW01130887

Praise for...
The Yellow Car

'Playful and important, *The Yellow Car* reminds us that we can constantly choose how to perceive and respond to the world. Powell puts us back in the driver's seat instead of letting our fears drive.'

Shawn Achor, New York Times bestselling author of *The Happiness Advantage*

'Insightful, freeing and funny, I loved *The Yellow Car.*'

Chip Conley, New York Times bestselling author of *Emotional Equations*

'*The Yellow Car* is a true life fable about not allowing unnecessary stress to rule our lives. With humour and self-deprecation, Toni Powell teaches us a new mantra to turn to when our molehills start feeling like mountains.'

Ben Lee, Songwriter and Musician

'I love *The Yellow Car*. With humour, insight and wisdom Toni gives us a great vehicle for change.'

Petrea King, author and founder, Quest for Life Centre

'This wise little book reminds us of what really matters. A delightful read!'

Jono Fisher, Founder of the Kindness Cards & WakeUpProject.com.au

'With a clever mix of insight, imagery, and humour, *The Yellow Car* drives home the keys to happiness.'

Barbara Fredrickson, Ph.D, author of *Positivity and Love 2.0*

'Whimsical and insightful... a true personal growth story that will have you question the small stuff and never, ever look at a yellow car the same way again.'

Eric Handler, Co-Founder of PositivelyPositive.com

'Sometimes the simplest stories make the most powerful points; and this is certainly true of Toni's *The Yellow Car*. What a great message for us all to heed!'

Prof Tim Sharp, aka Dr Happy

The Yellow Car

How I stopped driving myself crazy

written by Toni Powell
illustrated by Philip & Toni Powell

Text copyright © Toni Powell, 2015
Illustration copyright © Philip and Toni Powell, 2015

Editing: Rose Allan
Book design: Helen Chapman & Toni Powell
Cover design: Helen Chapman

1st Edition, June 2015

Published by:
P & T Powell
PO Box 232
Bli Bli, Qld 4560
Australia

The moral right of the author and illustrators has been asserted. All rights reserved. Without limiting the rights under copyright reserved above, no part of the publication may be reproduced, stored in or introduced into a retrieval system, or transmitted in any form or by any means (electronic, mechanical, photocopying, recording or otherwise) without the prior written permission of the copyright owner.

ISBN 978-0-9942960-3-0

Printed in Australia on environmentally friendly paper.

DEDICATION

To my beautiful mother Evelyn.

I am the luckiest of daughters to have you for my mother. Your generosity in all things amazes me. Your belief and support made this book possible.

Late one night, in a quiet suburban street, a yellow car drove into my life and changed it.

This is the story of what happened...

The Yellow Car

I breathe a sigh of relief when we arrive safely at the home of our friends, Mark and Karen. It's 10 pm and I'm not the calmest of passengers. In fact the only reason my husband, Phil, and I are even staying overnight in town is my fear. I worry we'll be killed in a car crash if we drive home late at night.

Fortunately he's an 'as you wish' kinda guy.

I can't wait to get in the door, up the stairs, kick off my shoes and relax. There's little I like more than hanging out with close friends.

We've been best friends for forty years and I'm expecting a warm and excited greeting.

Perhaps, "How fabulous to see your divine faces" or something equally suited to our 'very-special-friends' status.

Instead, when Karen opens the door her first words are –

" You didn't park your
car on the nature strip over
the road did you? "

While I wonder why parking over the road could be an issue, Phil reassures Karen that our car is in her driveway.

In the ensuing hugs and chatter I forget to ask what the problem was.

I won't have long to wait for an answer though.

We go upstairs talking excitedly, calling out for Mark to pour the wine. We're just about to start our evening of fun when we hear violent pounding coming from downstairs. Our eyebrows shoot up in collective alarm.

Bang, bang, bang. There it goes again.

"Sounds like one very angry person out there," Phil says.

We look around at each other hoping for an explanation. I offer my best guess, "Axe murderer?" but Mark is pretty sure they don't knock.

We can't agree on who should go down to face certain death, so all four of us gingerly descend the stairs.

Karen opens the door to reveal an irate woman. The woman takes a step inside, looks straight at Phil, and barks -

"Is that *your* car on *my* nature strip?"

Through the door I can see a little yellow car parked on the grass across the street. "Her nature strip?" I think, "Hers? It's public property." Given her obviously volatile state, I keep my thoughts to myself.

Phil assures her that the car isn't ours. I don't think she believes him because she carries on interrogating us.

Eventually she leaves, convinced I'm sure, that we aren't to be trusted.

The door has barely closed before we start sniggering like naughty children. There's nothing like a bit of neighbourhood nuttiness to kick off an evening.

Still giggling, we head back upstairs. Mark pours the wine and we take our glasses out to the front verandah.

It's a beautiful balmy night and I settle in for one of our treasured evenings of deep conversation.

Our discussion doesn't last long.

Very conveniently, as it turns out, Mark and Karen's verandah affords a bird's eye view of the house with the yellow car out front.

Sipping my wine, I glance over the railing and see an extraordinary scene.

After a few minutes I call everyone over to watch the drama unfolding in the street.

The irate woman and a clearly upset man (her husband, says Karen) are walking round and round the car we'd seen earlier.

As she circles the car the woman pulls roughly on the door handles – each one in turn. He tries to open the boot and even attempts to push the car.

I'm astounded. Are they trying to break into a car that isn't theirs? Their interaction with the car is anything but civil.

We lean on the railing, watching as the couple continues this odd behaviour. After ten minutes or so they leave the car and disappear inside the house. I'm dismayed the show is over.

But no!

To my great delight the couple come back out the door. They start talking in an agitated manner and begin to pace back and forth on their small verandah.

We are spellbound.

As they discuss whatever it is they're discussing, they wave their arms around. They both stop pacing – she to stare at the car – he to make, what seems to be, a rather distressed call.

Mark speculates, "Who can that guy be calling about a car at this hour?"

I watch all this with growing glee.

Our very own street opera ... and we've got box seats.

You're probably imagining that these people are old and have little to do but obsess about the minutiae of life and the sins of their neighbours.

Let me rid your mind of that picture, this couple are not in their eighties – or their seventies, sixties, fifties, forties – or even their thirties.

They are in their late twenties and this is –

Friday night

As everyone knows, most people in their twenties, on a Friday night, are at the pub, at a party, at a friend's place or doing something wildly exciting.

Or, if they aren't adventurous types, they'd go out to dinner, have friends over, see a movie, or even watch a video at home. At the very least they'd be having some fun in bed together.

Surely this couple can find something more enjoyable to do on a Friday night than harass a harmless little yellow car?

To our astonishment the couple come out through the front gate and begin their wondrous performance all over again.

They circle the car. They yank at handles. They kick the tyres. Then, they go back to the verandah and start the pacing afresh.

It's as if we've pressed replay.

He goes inside and we can clearly see him walking up and down the corridor.

When he comes out he stands in the front doorway, puts his arm high against the doorframe and leans his head on his arm – as if there's tragedy afoot.

He's a perfect
silhouette of anguish.

We're doubled over with laughter, tears running down our faces. This crazy couple has spent the best part of an hour fretting about a car parked on public property outside their house.

I'm thinking, "This is hilarious, who would be that stupid? Who would waste their Friday night upset about a car?"

Through my laughter I gasp, "Who, who, who, would do this?"

And then I stop laughing.

I'm having an epiphany.

Right now, in the suburbs, on an ordinary night.

Suddenly I know exactly who behaves like this. With sickening clarity I know who is as idiotic as this couple.

ME!

I would be this stupid.

I am this stupid.

My own life is being
enacted out before me
in this suburban street.

I stare down at this couple throwing their absurd tantrum, prancing up and down, their arms akimbo, their unhappiness leaking down the road.

It's as if I'm staring into a mirror.

This is exactly what I do when things are unfair, or if I say something stupid. This is exactly what I do when the future seems uncertain.

I go round and round whatever yellow car happens to be parked outside my house – no matter how long it's been there – tugging on worry, kicking at problems, pacing and pacing.

I try to leave the car alone but before I know it I'm out the gate –

... yanking on doors again.

I suddenly understand that I've been driving myself crazy with my fears, imagined catastrophes, regrets and obsessions.

With a sinking heart I realise I've been driving everyone around me crazy too. I close my eyes and see me on the phone, hundreds of times, rehashing that past hurt, freaking out about the future or whining about what went wrong.

With my sorry tales I'm painting a picture of tragedy each day.

I'm just like the crazy couple.

I am them.

I hug my misery and hang on tight, unwilling to let it go – even on a Friday night…

After a few moments of sobering enlightenment, I say to Phil, "Whenever I start doing that – whenever I start acting in that insane way about something that happened previously, that I can't do anything about. Or some imagined something that might happen in the future – remind me about tonight. Just say the words –

'It's a yellow car

so I remember this moment."

Phil laughs, pulls me close and kisses the tip of my nose. He's clearly delighted that I've finally noticed my crazy behaviour.

He leans in further and whispers in my ear,

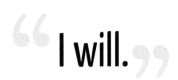 "I will."

Saturday.

I wake up thinking about the yellow car; I'm enjoying the fact that a moment of great insight happened in the midst of such delicious laughter.

I smile to myself and jump out of bed eager to see if the car is still in the street.

It's gone.

I can't help feeling a little wistful and I'm dying to know what happened to it.

Over breakfast we amuse ourselves with increasingly ridiculous theories about the car's disappearance.

"I bet they got it towed," Karen begins.

Phil's explanation is the silliest and involves a chainsaw, a bonfire and a backyard burial. He's clearly watched too many murder mysteries.

We're still laughing when Ryan, Mark and Karen's son, joins us. We recount, what has already become, 'The Story of The Yellow Car' and are thrilled when Ryan is able to fill in the rest of the tale.

Around midnight, after we'd all gone to bed, Ryan and some of his friends arrived home from a concert. They'd barely stepped out of their cars when the couple came out and started haranguing them with a string of questions.

"Is this your car?"

"What's it doing here?"

"Who owns it?"

Ryan and his friends denied any knowledge of cars, yellow or otherwise, and then quickly retreated to the safety of the house.

However they weren't being strictly honest. They were well aware that a friend of Ryan's owns the yellow car.

Ryan tells us that at around 3 am his friend arrived to collect her vehicle. She simply unlocked the door, started it up… and drove the car away.

As I ponder the little yellow car disappearing quietly into the night I'm reminded of the many things I've freaked out about, fretted about, stressed about, and carried on about.

In another profound 'aha' moment I realise most of them have also just disappeared of their own accord.

All the worrying I've
done hasn't affected the
outcome at all.

EPILOGUE

It's been a few years since my suburban epiphany. Years that have been full of financial uncertainty, unemployment, relationship agony, high stress situations and many real and imagined worries.

They could easily have been tough, sad, hard years.

Instead, these were the years where I discovered that remaining calm is a shelter from storms and that letting go equals lightheartedness. Thanks to the yellow car and large doses of gratitude (for all of life's wonders) these have been some of my happiest years.

I have a suspicion that all my family and friends, especially Phil, are eternally grateful to that car.

The yellow car has changed how I do life.

I keep a picture of one on my fridge and another on my computer. Just a glance at them is usually sufficient to remind me of the insanity of my thoughts or behaviour.

Failing that I can always count on Phil to whisper (or yell) –

"It's **just** a yellow car!"

And then I laugh.

60

ADDENDUM

This story took place in a hilly, green and leafy suburb of Brisbane.

Mark and Karen still live opposite the couple who continue to harass cars of all colours on any given day of the week.

Whenever I visit I'm sorely tempted to park on their nature strip (I know!).

Thanks, thanks, thanks

to the many friends of *The Yellow Car* who
helped get it on the road and over the humps.

The content of the book owes so much to the loving input of my clever editor **Rose** Allan, my creative, patient friends **Mary-Lou** and **Mark**, and my sister **Angela**. My magic graphic designer, **Helen** Chapman, added the zing.

Suzy Wilson of Riverbend Books in Brisbane, **Annie** Grossman of Annie's Books in Peregian, **Mary-Lou** Stephens, **Aishah** Macgill, **Siobahn** Barter, **Lara** Masselos, **Beth** Phelan, **Neil** Roberts, **Ian** Baistow, **Leslie** Reed, **Joe** McFeeters, **Leigh** Inglis, **Sean** Andrews and **Gerhard** Grossmann – I had written about the specific contribution each of you made until **Mary-Lou** pointed out that (hilariously) the thanks were longer than the book. I culled. Suffice to say that your generous gifts are deeply treasured.

Special thanks to

My wildly wonderful children, **Hailey**, **Isaac**, **Nick**, **Georgia** and **Bene** and their delicious families – you make me smile, give me cause for gratitude and provide me interesting 'yellow cars'. You are my teachers, my wealth, my heart and I adore you. Your input, patience and care toward this book has deeply touched me.

Angela, my incredible sister, you are so special, your advice so timely. Your huge heart makes other people's dreams come true (mine included).

Pamela, your love, belief and generosity stopped me from scrapping this book. **Karen**, you have the best weird neighbours and are the most hospitable, kind and tolerant person I know. **Mark**, your wisdom improves my life and my books. You are, all three, the dearest of long devoted friends.

Philip, my darling man, you were willing to lay everything on the line, put up with me, work crazy hours and learn a host of new skills to make *The Yellow Car* a reality. I love you beyond words.

About the Author

Toni Powell has been on a quest to find simple ways to bring joy and contentment into her life. Her search has found her picking the brains of ridiculously happy people and mind-boffins from around the world. Being a storyteller at heart, Toni takes all she learns and turns it into entertaining talks and classes that she shares at conferences, in schools, at work places and online. She's made two award-winning short films and is currently working on a documentary about gratitude called *Goodness Gracious Me!* Toni has been the subject of an inspiring episode of ABC's *Australian Story* called *'Let There Be Light'.*

About the Illustrators

From the moment they got together in the back seat of a Volkswagen the pairing of Philip and Toni has been a fruitful one – five kids for a start.

Undaunted by inexperience, the Powells will tackle anything that might be a fun way to help people enjoy life more.

Their adventures include founding a 'feel good' international film festival, filming a documentary, producing a life-changing online video series *The Great Full Life Class* and contributing DNA to a hoard of grandchildren.

In this latest collaboration, the Powells have ventured into new territory and wedded Phil's craftsman/engineering expertise with Toni's budding drawing skills to bring *The Yellow Car* story to life.

VISIT

www.tonipowell.me/sowhatnow
for simple **free** ways to wipe frowns off faces.
(hint: send your friends there if they're
driving themselves crazy).

INVITE: Toni to speak at your event
speaker@tonipowell.me

WEBSITE: To learn more check out
tonipowell.me

Lightning Source UK Ltd.
Milton Keynes UK
UKHW050426170920
370021UK00003B/33